INCREDIBLE BASKETBALL RECORDS

BY TYLER MASON

Published by The Child's World®
1980 Lookout Drive • Mankato, MN 56003-1705
800-599-READ • www.childsworld.com

Acknowledgments
The Child's World®: Mary Swensen, Publishing Director
Red Line Editorial: Editorial direction and production
The Design Lab: Design

Photographs ©: Lightspring/Shutterstock Images, cover, 1, 2, 23; Mike Cooper/
Allsport/Getty Images, 5; Ben Margot/AP Images, 6; Mark Halmas/Icon Sportswire, 9;
Marcio Jose Sanchez/AP Images, 10, 20; Steve Lipofsky/Corbis, 13, 17; Bettmann/
Corbis, 14, 16; Tom DiPace/AP Images, 19

Design Elements: Shutterstock Images

ISBN 9781503808874
LCCN 2015958446

Printed in the United States of America
Mankato, MN
June, 2016
PA02307

TABLE OF CONTENTS

CHAPTER 1

SINGLE-GAME RECORDS

MOST REBOUNDS
55 Rebounds
Wilt Chamberlain • Philadelphia Warriors
November 24, 1960

Wilt Chamberlain was a great rebounder. The Philadelphia Warriors center set the single-game **rebound** record in his second season in the National Basketball Association (NBA). The record had been held by Boston Celtics center Bill Russell. Russell grabbed 51 rebounds in a game just nine months earlier. Chamberlain set the record against Russell and the Celtics. Chamberlain also scored 34 points that night. He averaged 27.2 rebounds that season.

MOST ASSISTS
30 Assists
Scott Skiles • Orlando Magic
December 30, 1990

The Orlando Magic beat the Denver Nuggets 155–116. But after the game, people only wanted to talk about Scott Skiles. The Magic's point guard set up his teammates for baskets all night long. Kevin Porter of the New Jersey Nets had set the old record of 29 **assists** in 1978. Skiles also scored 22 points in the victory. He averaged 8.4 assists per game that year. Skiles became Orlando's coach in 2015.

SCOTT SKILES

MOST POINTS IN A QUARTER
37 Points
Klay Thompson • Golden State Warriors
January 23, 2015

Golden State Warriors guard Klay Thompson was on fire. He scored 52 points in a game against the Sacramento Kings. In the third **quarter** Thompson made history. He made all 13 of his shots in the quarter. Nine of them were **three-pointers**. He added two **free throws**. The Warriors scored 41 points in that quarter. Thompson had 37 of them. No NBA player had ever scored more than 33 points in a quarter.

MOST FIELD GOALS WITHOUT A MISS

18 Field Goals

Wilt Chamberlain • Philadelphia 76ers
February 26, 1967

Wilt Chamberlain set many NBA records. One night he took 18 shots and he made all 18 of them. Chamberlain also made six free throws. He scored 42 points that night for the Philadelphia 76ers. In the same season, "Wilt the Stilt" had two other perfect shooting nights. He made all 15 of his shots in one game and all 16 in another.

WILT GOES WILD

One of Wilt Chamberlain's records might never be broken. He scored 100 points in a game on March 2, 1962. No player has come close since then. Los Angeles Lakers guard Kobe Bryant scored 81 points in a 2006 game. He is the only other NBA player to have scored at least 80 points in a game.

CHAPTER 2

SINGLE-SEASON RECORDS

MOST BLOCKED SHOTS
456 Blocked Shots
Mark Eaton • Utah Jazz

Mark Eaton towered over his opponents. He stood 7 feet 4 inches tall. He guarded the basket for the Utah Jazz for 11 years. Eaton blocked 456 shots in the 1984–85 season. That is an average of 5.6 **blocked shots** per game. Only one other player has blocked 400 shots in a season. Eaton finished his career with 3,064 blocks.

HIGHEST FREE-THROW PERCENTAGE
98.1 Percent
José Calderón • Toronto Raptors

In the 2008–09 season, José Calderón was nearly perfect from the free-throw line. The Toronto Raptors guard shot 154 free throws that year. He missed only three. No player who had shot at least 125 free throws in any season had done better. The old record was 95.8 percent. Calderón's longest streak that season was 87 in a row.

JOSÉ CALDERÓN

STEPHEN CURRY

MOST THREE-POINT BASKETS
402 Three-Point Baskets
Stephen Curry • Golden State Warriors

Stephen Curry is a sharpshooter from long distance. He's a threat to make a shot from almost anywhere on the court. In the 2015–16 season, Curry shattered the record for most three-point baskets in a season. He held the old record, too, with 286 three-pointers. He passed that with 24 games left in the season. But he kept on shooting. Curry made 10 of 19 three-point attempts in his last game of the season. It was the fourth time he'd made at least 10 three-pointers in a game that year.

MOST TRIPLE-DOUBLES
41 Triple-Doubles
Oscar Robertson • Cincinnati Royals

A triple-double is when one player reaches double figures (at least 10) in three main statistical categories—usually points, rebounds, and assists. Cincinnati Royals guard Oscar Robertson did that an amazing 41 times in the 1961–62 season. Robertson was the only player in NBA history to average a triple-double for an entire season. He finished the 1961–62 season with single-game averages of 30.8 points, 12.5 rebounds, and 11.4 assists.

BELLAMY'S BIG SEASON

Each NBA team plays 82 games in the regular season. But Hall of Fame center Walt Bellamy played in 88 games in the 1968–69 season. He played 35 games with the New York Knicks before he was traded to the Detroit Pistons. They had only played 29 games at that point in the season. Bellamy played in the rest to set the record.

CHAPTER 3

CAREER RECORDS

MOST ASSISTS
15,806 Assists
John Stockton

For 19 seasons, John Stockton was a brilliant point guard for the Utah Jazz. He ended his career in 2003 with more assists than any player in NBA history. Jason Kidd is second with almost 4,000 fewer assists. Stockton led the league in assists for nine straight seasons. He averaged 10.5 assists per game in his career. Stockton was a 10-time All-Star and is in the Basketball Hall of Fame.

MOST GAMES PLAYED
1,611 Games
Robert Parish

Longtime Boston Celtics center Robert Parish played 21 NBA seasons. He was 43 years old when he retired. Parish's total does not include his 184 playoff games or nine All-Star Games. He played in 51 more games than Los Angeles Lakers great Kareem Abdul-Jabbar.

ROBERT PARISH

13

WILT CHAMBERLAIN

MOST REBOUNDS
23,924 Rebounds
Wilt Chamberlain

Wilt Chamberlain was the best rebounder in NBA history. He led the league in rebounding 11 times. He averaged 22.9 rebounds per game in his 14-year career. Chamberlain's season high for rebounds was 2,149. He did that in 1960–61. Chamberlain's longtime **rival** Bill Russell is second. Russell grabbed 21,620 rebounds in 13 seasons.

MOST POINTS IN THE NBA FINALS

1,679 Points

Jerry West

Point guard Jerry West led the Los Angeles Lakers to the NBA playoffs 13 times. They won the NBA championship in 1972. West scored 1,679 career points in the NBA Finals. Kareem Abdul-Jabbar is next with 1,317 points. West retired in 1974. He was an All-Star in all 14 of his seasons.

HIGH-SCORING CENTER

Kareem Abdul-Jabbar could score a lot of ways. He was famous for his hook shot. He also could dunk. And he shot a lot of free throws. Abdul-Jabbar played 20 seasons in the NBA. He scored 38,387 career points. That is the most of any NBA player. Abdul-Jabbar averaged 24.6 points per game in his career.

MOST NBA CHAMPIONSHIPS FOR ONE PLAYER
11 Championships
Bill Russell

Bill Russell has more championship rings than fingers. He played 13 seasons with the Boston Celtics. Russell won 11 NBA championships. His first championship came in the 1956–57 season. He was a rookie. The Celtics won eight straight titles. Russell won his 11th championship in 1969. It was his final season. Sam Jones was Russell's teammate for most of his career. Jones won 10 NBA championships.

MOST SEASONS LEADING THE LEAGUE IN SCORING
10 Seasons
Michael Jordan

The great Michael Jordan played 15 NBA seasons. He led the league in scoring in 10 of them. His first scoring title came in 1986–87, his third NBA season. He scored 37.1 points per game that year. That also was his career high. Wilt Chamberlain had the record before Jordan broke it. Chamberlain led the league in scoring seven times.

MICHAEL JORDAN

CHAPTER 4

TEAM RECORDS

LONGEST WINNING STREAK
33 Games
1971–72 Los Angeles Lakers

The Chicago Bulls broke one important record held by the 1971–72 Lakers (see next page). But Los Angeles still has the longest winning streak. It began with a win on November 5, 1971. Los Angeles won 33 straight games. Finally the Milwaukee Bucks beat them on January 9, 1972. That Lakers team won the NBA Finals.

MOST NBA FINALS APPEARANCES WITHOUT A LOSS

6 Appearances
Chicago Bulls

The Chicago Bulls have gone to the NBA Finals six times. They've won them all. The Bulls won all six of their NBA titles in the 1990s. They won three in a row from 1990–91 to 1992–93. Then after two years falling short of the NBA Finals, they won three more in a row.

The 1995–96 team was probably their best. Chicago won 72 of 82 games that year. Michael Jordan averaged 30.4 points per game. He won the NBA Most Valuable Player Award. Jordan and Scottie Pippen started for the Eastern Conference in the All-Star Game. Phil Jackson was Chicago's coach for all six of the Bulls' titles.

SCOTTIE PIPPEN

MOST VICTORIES IN A SEASON
73 Victories
2015–16 Golden State Warriors

The Golden State Warriors had history in their sights from the start of the 2015–16 season. They started out with 24 straight wins, setting an NBA record. No team had ever won more than 15 straight games to start a season. But they were just getting started. The Warriors finished the year 73–9, breaking the record of the 1995–96 Chicago Bulls, who went 72–10. Golden State coach Steve Kerr was a member of that Bulls team.

MOST POINTS IN A GAME BY ONE TEAM

186 Points

Detroit Pistons

The Pistons traveled to Denver and beat the Nuggets 186–184 on December 13, 1983. The game went to triple **overtime**. Both teams broke the old record of 173 points in a game. The game was tied 145–145 at the end of regulation. Denver's Kiki Vandeweghe led all scorers with 51 points. Isiah Thomas scored 47 points for the Pistons.

FAIL-ADELPHIA

While the Warriors were setting a record for hottest start to a season, the Philadelphia 76ers were doing just the opposite. The Sixers lost their first 18 games of the 2015–16 season. That tied the 2009–10 New Jersey Nets for the worst start to a season in NBA history.

GLOSSARY

assist (uh-SISST): An assist is a pass that leads to a made basket. John Stockton led the NBA in assists nine times.

blocked shot (BLOKD SHOT): A blocked shot happens when a defensive player prevents a shot from getting to the basket by knocking it out of the air. Mark Eaton had a lot of blocked shots.

free throw (FREE THROH): A free throw is an unguarded shot taken from a line 15 feet (4.6 m) from the basket. Micheal Williams made most of his free throws.

overtime (OH-vur-time): Overtime is an extra period played to determine a winner if the score is tied at the end of regulation. The Pistons and Nuggets played three overtime periods.

quarter (KWOR-tur): A quarter is one of four 12-minute periods of playing time in a game. Klay Thompson scored 37 points in one quarter.

rebound (REE-bound): A rebound happens when a player grabs the ball after a missed shot. Wilt Chamberlain averaged more rebounds in a season than any player in NBA history.

rival (RYE-vuhl): A rival is an opponent with whom a player or team has a fierce and ongoing competition. Bill Russell's rival was Wilt Chamberlain.

three-pointer (THREE-POINT-ur): A three-pointer is shot that is made from behind the three-point line. Stephen Curry makes a lot of three-pointers.

IN THE LIBRARY

Rausch, David. *National Basketball Association.*
Minneapolis, MN: Bellwether Media, 2015.

Schaller, Bob, and Dave Harnish. *The Everything Kids'*
Basketball Book. Avon, MA: Adams Media, 2009.

Winters, Jaime. *Center Court: The History of Basketball.*
New York: Crabtree Publishing, 2016.

ON THE WEB

Visit our Web site for links about basketball: **childsworld.com/links**

Note to Parents, Teachers, and Librarians: We routinely verify our Web links to make sure they are safe and active sites. So encourage your readers to check them out!

INDEX

ABOUT THE AUTHOR

Tyler Mason studied journalism at the University of Wisconsin-Madison, where he won the 2008 Big Ten Conference William R. Reed Memorial Award for student journalism. He has covered professional and college sports in Minneapolis and St. Paul, Minnesota, since 2009. He currently lives in Hudson, Wisconsin, with his wife.